THOUGHTS ON GENESIS

A COMMENTARY BY:

WALKER LANE

WALKER LANE

Dedication

I dedicate this book to all those who search the scriptures and to God Who removed the scales from my eyes.

INTRODUCTION

Dear Reader:

It is believed that Genesis was written by Moses in the 1400s B.C. It is the first book of the Bible. By definition, the word genesis means *beginning*. This book is a commentary of Genesis derived from years of study and reflection.

The Bible speaks different things at different times, yet never changes. The very verse you have read a thousand times in confusion may suddenly make sense at a different time in your life. It is a living, breathing work from our Lord to us. There is no substitute for the reading of the actual, physical Word of God, but it's always nice to explore other's thoughts on the verses too. These are my thoughts. Thank you for reading them. If you have any questions or would like to share your insights, please email me at walkerlane55@gmail.com.

Stay in the Word,

Walker Lane

CONTENTS

GENESIS 1-3

Genesis 1:1-2

In the beginning God created the heavens and the earth. The earth was formless and void, and darkness was over the surface of the deep, and the Spirit of God was moving over the surface of the waters. Genesis 1:1-2

I wonder how many Bible readers actually notice that all of this happened BEFORE the first day. The earth could have been billions of years old before God created light, and wasn't it the light that marked the first day? Maybe the light just started the calendar of time, but not the existence of the earth. So, maybe scientists were right about the earth (dirt) being 4.54 billion years old—give or take 50 million years, of course.

Genesis 1:1-Genesis 2:7

Remember that God had already formed the earth (which is made of dust) before the first day, leaving us to wonder just how old the earth could really be. Please go find your bible, dust it off (pun intended), and read the verses, or you can look them up on the internet. God created all kinds of good stuff the first few days:

Day 1: Light. God separated day from night.

Day 2: God created an expanse (heaven) between the waters, placing some water above the sky and the rest of the water below it on the earth.

Day 3: God gathered the earthly water together to let dry land appear. He also created sprouting vegetation, plants yielding seed, and fruit trees bearing seed in the fruits so they would grow more trees.

Day 4: God created the sun, moon, and stars to provide light, to mark signs and seasons, and to separate day from night.

Day 5: God created the creatures of the sea and the birds in the air.

Day 6: God created living creatures on the earth, then He created man.

Day 7: God rested and blessed the seventh day and sanctified it.

Verse 1:26, *Then God said, "Let Us make man in Our image, according to Our likeness..."* Here we are introduced to the Holy Trinity: Father, Son, Holy Spirit. Jesus was up there right along with God from the very beginning, as was the Holy Spirit. Gen. 2:7, *Then the Lord God formed man of dust from the ground.* If God used really old dust (remember, the earth had already been formed BEFORE the first day), then wouldn't that make the ingredients of man really old too? So though man was newly created, the dirt used to create him could be carbon dated as being much older. This seems to be a fairly logical explanation to the Christian quandary of the age of the earth.

Genesis 2:8 – Genesis 3:7

In these verses, God plants a garden toward the east in Eden and tells Adam to cultivate it. God created the trees to grow for food, for life, and *for*-bidden (the tree of the knowledge of good and evil). There are rivers to water the garden. He creates Eve to be a helpmate to Adam. He really only gives them one rule: *Do not eat from the tree of the knowledge of good and evil, for if you do, you will surely die.*

Did God just put the tree there to taunt them? Or did he forbid them to eat of it because He knew it would be bad for them? Well, they did eat from it, thanks to Eve being tricked by that darn snake, but they didn't die on that day, instead, their clock began ticking like a time bomb.

That was the day they started the aging and dying process. One thing I have learned in life is that activities which are labeled sin are labeled that way because of the harm they cause. It's kind of like putting a Mr. Yuck sticker on bleach bottles and other household cleaners so that our kids will know to steer clear. I don't believe God created rules just to be mean or to withhold the good stuff from us. Is that why you say no to your kids? Just like a good parent, He is trying to warn us that our sins can and will cause harm, not only to others, but to ourselves.

The choice has always been there from the very beginning. God sets before us two choices: life or death—the tree of life or the tree of the knowledge of good and evil. God gave us free will to choose. Eve made the wrong choice when she trusted the serpent over God. Then, since misery loves company, she dragged her poor husband right into the thick of it with her. By the way, he sure did throw her under the bus, didn't he? (Gen. 3:12). The wages of sin is death, but lucky for us, the free gift of God is eternal life in Jesus. Here's the thing, you have to choose whether or not to accept the gift, because God gave you free will. Eternity is a long time. Choose wisely.

Genesis 3:8 – 24

After Eve was deceived by the serpent, and she and Adam disobeyed God, they must have realized right away that they had done something wrong. They were either afraid or feeling guilty or both, and they hid from God. At one time or another, haven't we all wanted to hide from God? We close our eyes to Him, tune him out for a while because we don't want to face the wrong we've done, or maybe we just don't want to stop sinning. However, there is no hiding from God, and we all must face the music eventually. Isn't forgiveness amazing? Once we confront our sin, we have a chance to be redeemed.

So back in the garden, God gets a hold of Adam and Eve and questions them. Adam blames Eve. Eve blames the serpent. What does God do? He punishes the serpent. He puts enmity between it and the woman (there is lots of enmity between women and snakes, right?). He also promises that her seed would bruise his seed on the head, and that his seed would bruise her seed on the heel.

He did bruise the heel of Jesus when He suffered on the cross, but Jesus bruised his head when he defeated him at the cross. Though Jesus suffered, though he was crucified, He won. What did He win? He won the souls of God's children. The devil can never have our souls as long as we have Jesus. Now, if you give up Jesus and reject Him...well, I guess you're on your own. Satan has descendants as well. Look around at all the evil in the world. Satan's seed is here, and like the serpent, they are tricky.

When the serpent tricked Eve, he wasn't the only one to get punished. Eve and all women were punished by painful childbirth. (Thanks Eve.) Adam was punished by having to work harder in order to provide food. They were kicked out of the Garden of Eden. They once had it easy, but they wanted more, and so they fell. We could all learn so much from this story. Life goes by so fast. Appreciate the gifts you have been given. Appreciate the ones who love you. Stop looking around the corner for something more when you already have all you need.

At the end of chapter three, we see that God makes garments for Adam and Eve to wear, as if to say, *I haven't left you in your time of trouble. Though you have caused this calamity and made your life harder, I am still providing.*

To sum it up:

God gives us rules for our own good.

We break those rules.

There are harmful consequences.

God is still with us.

GENESIS 4-6

Genesis 4:1-8

Adam had relations with his wife Eve, and she gave birth to Cain, then she gave birth to Abel. Abel kept flocks of sheep, and Cain was a tiller of the ground. Cain brought an offering to the Lord of the fruit of the ground. Abel brought of the "firstlings" of his flock and of their fat portions as an offering to the Lord (fat was a good thing back then).

God didn't care for Cain's offering. I always wondered why. They both brought offerings. What was the problem? Does God not like vegetables? Well, I finally noticed what the problem was: According to the KJV bible, *In process of time it came to pass that Cain brought of the fruit of the ground,* but Abel brought of his "firstlings" (his first—the good stuff). *In the process of time...it came to pass*—It apparently took Cain a while, plus he brought fruit that had dropped to the ground. Therefore, he must not have brought from his first fruits, the best fruit, but brought the bruised fruit that had fallen to the ground.

Now we know from instructions to the Israelites later on in the bible, that they were to bring the first of their flock, not the last, so maybe Cain didn't give his first/his best; maybe he didn't follow the Lord's instructions. Unfortunately, the fact that God liked Abel's offering better angered Cain and he became jealous of his brother, so he killed him. Not exactly a good reason to kill your brother. I'm guessing there's more to that story.

In verse 6, God asks Cain why he's so angry. *If thou doest well, shalt thou not be accepted? And if thou doest not well, sin lieth at the door.* And if sin lieth at your door, you become sin's desire, but you must rule over it, instead of it ruling over you. It seems that once we open the door to that one little sin (Cain's lack of a worthy offering), it flings wide open to more sin (Cain's jealousy), and before we know it we have plunged right in (Abel's murder). It's sort of like the phrase *One lie leads to another.* It's better to keep that door closed on sin, even though that's not exactly easy.

1 John 3:12 states that Cain was of the evil one, and he slew his brother because his deeds were evil, and his brother's were righteous. The next verse warns us not to be surprised if the world hates us. Evil hates righteousness. That explains a lot, doesn't it?

Genesis 4:9-15

Cain has just killed his brother Abel, apparently over petty jealousy. In verse 9 God questions Cain, and Cain lies to God. Can you imagine lying to God? God asks you a question, and you know God knows EVERYTHING, but you still lie to Him? What sense does that make? Anyway, God asks Cain where his brother is, even though He already knows the answer. *The voice of thy brother's blood crieth unto Me from the ground.* BUSTED! So God curses Cain so that he can no longer yield fruit from the ground, and tells him he will be a vagrant and wanderer on the earth.

Did Cain feel bad? Did he say he was sorry? Not really. He actually told God his punishment was too harsh. Really? He told God he was worried someone might try to kill him. Ahhhhh, poor Cain. It's hard to feel sorry for him. He murders his own brother, doesn't seem to feel bad about it, but whines to God that his punishment is too harsh and he's scared someone might kill him—but our God is good, so what does He do? He promises that anyone who kills Cain, vengeance will be taken on him sevenfold, and then He set a mark upon Cain so that no one would kill him.

Does this mean that God still loved Cain? After all, He did provide him protection. It seems to me that God loves His children, whether or not they love Him back. However, God will not force us into Heaven. He will not open the pearly gates to everyone, even though He loves us all. The Bible says He will condemn Satan to hell, but gives everyone else a choice. However, we still need to make that choice on our own. I've heard people say that a loving god would never condemn His children to hell. He's not the One condemning souls to hell. People do that all on their own. So, have you made your choice yet? Do you know someone who hasn't? Send them the seed of knowledge and let God water it. Who knows...it might just save their soul.

Genesis 4: 16-26

Cain has killed his brother Abel, and God sends him out to wander the earth. Cain ends up in the land of Nod, which is east of Eden. This verse always seems to stump people. If Adam and Eve were the first people, and they only had two children (sons) and one was already dead, then how on earth could there be a city for Cain to go to? Well, my Bible says "*land* of Nod," not city, not territory, not community, just land, so this tells me that there is no reason to think it was already populated. BUT the next verse is confusing also, "Cain had relations with his wife." So where did she come from??? Well, the Bible doesn't say he met his wife in Nod, it just says he went there and he "knew/had relations with" his wife. So, either Cain's wife came from his rib (like Eve came from Adam), or Cain married a sister that had not been previously mentioned (Ewww! I like the rib idea better). We really don't know.

At any rate, they had a son called Enoch (not the same Enoch that God takes up into Heaven in verse 5:24). Then

Cain "built a city" (so it must not have already been there to begin with) and named it Enoch. On down the line they went—some of his descendants were not so virtuous. One of them was also a murderer and even had two wives.

Eve had another son, Seth, and he had a son called Enosh. Then men began to call upon the name of the Lord. Does this mean that the line of Cain did not call upon the name of the Lord? That would make sense. After all, Cain was none too pleased with God, so maybe he didn't teach his son to worship God, which would mean he couldn't teach his children to worship God either. After Seth is born and his descendants are listed, I don't see anything else written about the descendants of Cain, but that's not to say that they aren't scattered about. *It's worth noting that Noah came from the line of Seth.

Sin began with the first two humans who were created in God's image. If they couldn't get it right, then how can we? I don't blame God for flooding the earth. Looking around now, I wonder why He puts up with humankind at all. The world has changed tremendously since I was a little girl. However, the Bible says that there is nothing new under the sun. The thing that stands out to me the most is not the rampant sin, but the hate that seems to have taken over the hearts of the people in the world. It's sad. The Bible says that God is love. Those who do not know God, can they love? I don't know, but I do know that they sure are missing out. So what do we have that they reject when they reject God? Help, hope, strength, peace, unconditional love...and forgiveness.

Genesis 5 covers the generations from Adam to Noah.

I will never forget the time when my son called me and said (without even a "Hi Mom."), "What happened to m' man Enoch?"

My response: "Huh?" I soon realized he was talking about Enoch in the Bible. The Bible is very brief about Enoch's demise. In fact, it's so brief it's easy to completely miss. From Genesis 5:1 through 5:23 we are introduced to each generation starting with Adam. We are told four details of each man: his name, his age at the birth of his first son, the number of years he lives after the birth of his first son, and his age at death (Except for Adam, in which we are told his age at the birth of Seth who is his third son).

Adam had Seth at age 130 years. Then he lived 800 more years and had other sons and daughters. So Adam lived 930 years, and he died.

Seth was 105 when he had Enosh. He lived 807 more years, had other sons and daughters, so his years were 912, and he died.

Then we are given the details of Enosh, Kenan, Mahalalel, Jared, and Enoch, who was the father of Methuselah and others. He lived to be 365. Verse 24 tells us *Enoch walked with God; and he was not, for God took him.*

The generations of Methuselah, Lamech, and Noah were listed after, and after each man's information was stated, "and he died" — except for Enoch. So, to repeat my son, "What happened to m' man Enoch?"

Well, apparently he never had to die. God just took him. Why? Because he walked with God. Didn't the others walk with God? Maybe— probably—we know that Noah did, but Enoch must have been special because we are told in two separate verses that *Enoch walked with God* (verses 22 and 24). Is it odd that God just took Enoch? Well, it's different, but it happened to Elijah in 2 Kings chapter 2 also, and in 1 Thessalonians 4:17, we are told that one day we will be caught up together in the clouds to meet the Lord in the air to always be with Him, so we know that it will happen again.

Now many people will say that the word "rapture" is not in the Bible, but the description of the Rapture, as Christians understand it, is in the Bible. It's very clear. The dead in Christ shall rise first then we who are alive and remain will be caught up together with them. This is what we know as the Rapture, and it is in the Bible. People have differing opinions on when the Rapture will take place. Will it be before the tribulation described in Revelation, mid-tribulation, or at the end of the tribulation? I just don't know.

Genesis 6:1-13 (Tricky Tricky)

Genesis Chapter 6 describes wicked times in the Bible and contains verses which are controversial due to the differing views of educated Bible scholars. Some Bible scholars believe that the sons of God mentioned in verse 2 are actually fallen angels who, with Satan, were thrown out of Heaven. Other Bible scholars believe that the sons of God are believers from the line of Seth (Adam and Eve's beloved son). Both arguments have merit. See why it's so tricky?

Some argue that fallen angels married humans and bore children who were mighty and well known. This union corrupted the DNA of man. I daresay, were the Greeks right? Is Greek mythology not a myth after all?

Supportive scripture:

Verse 2: The King James Version states that the sons of God saw the daughters of men—that they were beautiful—and took them as wives.

Verse 4: There were giants in the earth in those days when the daughters of man bore children to the sons of God—the same became mighty men, legends.

Verse 5: The wickedness of man was great and continually evil.

Verse 12 and 13: The earth was corrupt and filled with violence and the flesh was corrupt, so God planned to destroy the earth and all flesh (except for Noah and his family).

Other versions of the Bible refer to the giants in verse 4 as Nephilim which means "the fallen ones". Another version just refers to them as "the fallen ones".

Verses alluding to or referencing the sons of God as angels:

Job 1:6 "...the sons of God came to present themselves before the Lord, and Satan came also among them."

Job 2:1 "Again there was a day when the sons of God came to present themselves before the Lord, and Satan came also among them to present himself before the Lord.

Job 38:7 God is questioning Job asking where he was when He (God) was creating the world, "...when the morning stars sang together, and all the sons of God shouted for joy," (KJV). The NIV refers to them as angels.

Jude 1:6-7 "...angels who did not keep their own domain, but abandoned their proper abode..." (6) "just as Sodom and Gomorrah and the cities around them, since they in the same way as these indulged in gross immorality and went after strange flesh."(7)

Verses referencing giants: Numbers 13:33, Deut. 2:20-21 and 3:11, 1 Samuel 17:4, 2 Samuel 21:15-22

Others argue that the sons of God are referring to the line of Seth.

Supportive Scripture:

Genesis 4:26: "...to Seth...Then men began to call upon the name of the Lord." Seth was a believer, a follower of God. His descendants were also believers. We are called the children of God, so Seth's line could have been referred to as the sons of God.

It is human beings led by God's Spirit who are called "sons of God" in:

(KJV) 1 John 3:1: "Behold, what manner of love the Father hath bestowed upon us, that we should be called the sons of God..."

Romans 8:14: "For as many as are led by the Spirit of God, they are the sons of God."

Galatians 4:6: "And because ye are sons, God hath sent forth the Spirit of his Son into your hearts, crying, Abba, Father."

2 Peter 1:20 tells us that no prophesy of scripture is a matter of one's own interpretation. There is a right answer

here. Honestly, I myself do not know what that answer may be. Sometimes the Bible seems cryptic and confusing, but in the end it really won't matter. All that will really matter is that I am a child of God who loves and accepts me, and Jesus has saved my soul. We won't understand everything that's in the Bible until we can ask God ourselves. Although, the Bible does say that all will be revealed in the end—and that's another fun topic.

Genesis 6:5-22

In Genesis 6:5-22, God revealed to Noah that He would destroy the earth because it was filled with violence. He saw that the wickedness of man was great and that his heart was continually evil; however, God saw goodness in Noah and spared him, his family, and the animals two by two.

God told Noah to build the ark (we all know the story) in order to survive. Noah did as he was told. It took him a long time to build the ark, but it also took a long time for God to act on His plan of destruction. Meanwhile, poor Noah must have looked the fool. After all, he probably spent all his time and hard-earned money building that ark, trying to get people to change their ways, and God was taking His own sweet time.

Poor Noah. People probably thought he was a nut for believing that God would actually destroy the world. I wonder if people said back then, *God is a loving god. God does not punish people. He saves everyone.* Isn't that what they say now? Well, I guess they are partially correct. God is loving, and He does save everyone who turns to Him to be saved, but that isn't everyone, is it? God did destroy man and earth. The overwhelming evil of man caused Him to do it. As in the days of Noah, it shall be again. History often repeats itself, and it will again.

Though God did promise He would never again flood the earth (remember the original meaning of the rainbow?), He also promises that He will one day destroy the wickedness of mankind again. Make no mistake, God will not be put off forever. I've heard preachers say that God did not cause Covid. I've also heard some say that He did. He is more than capable of bringing down plagues (remember Exodus?). God will do what He does. How do we know whether He did or didn't? Well, my guess is that the devil is the one causing most of the trouble down here; God just uses that trouble for good (and we have seen that too, in abundance).

So, here we are as in the days of Noah, where men continually seek out wickedness, where God is continually rejected by so many. Like Noah, some people think we (Christians) are just nuts, so we may long for the day when we can say "I told ya so," all the while dreading the day when our faith is proven right, because sadly, not all of our loved ones will be saved with us. The good news is, there is still time for the lost to be saved, but don't hesitate to help them find Christ, for we do not know how much time, do we?

GENESIS 7-9

Genesis 7 – 8:4

In chapter six, God told Noah to build the ark, and he did, as crazy as it must have seemed. God found Noah to be righteous and wanted to save him and his family. He was 600 years old when God began to send rain upon the earth with a promise to blot out every remaining living thing. 40 days and 40 nights, fountains of the great deep burst forth from the earth colluding with the pouring-down rain to destroy God's creation. There was so much water that even the mountains were covered. After 150 days it finally receded, and the ark ended up safely parked on the mountains of Ararat.

Most of us have heard the story of Noah and the flood. Even many non-Christian cultures believe there was once a great flood that covered the earth. God, who created earth, man, and all living things was disgusted enough to destroy His own creation. Why? Just like now, His own creation rejected Him, seeking their own harmful pleasures. Then He sent Jesus, His Son, to take the punishment for our sins, and the world rejected Him again. How long will God take it? How long will He allow his creation to shake their fists at Him? Where has fear of the Lord gone?

Christians shouldn't fear God, right? Well, fear is the beginning of wisdom (Proverbs 9:10). Many sinners initially come to Christ because of fear and shame. Fear gets them to sit up and take notice. Fear gets them in the door. God should be feared if you aren't saved. He destroyed the earth once. What makes you think He won't do it again? Matthew 10:34 says He has come with a sword, and in the end He will be back with the sword—not tolerance.

Only as Christians mature in the faith is fear replaced with understanding. God loves us. He wants us. He is a jealous God. He won't share. He also won't force you to choose Him. He doesn't want your love through a love potion; He wants your genuine love. The choice is either God or Satan. There is no in between. If you don't choose God (the One who created you), you have by default chosen Satan. Where do you think the evil ones end up in the end? Many don't believe in Hell, but that doesn't mean it doesn't exist. Be careful of the choices you make now; the consequences will be eternal.

If you feel God in your heart calling out to you, but you don't know what to do, reach for the Bible, and reach out to someone you know who belongs to Christ. The way is simple and so much better than what the world has to offer. Don't delay, not just so you can go to Heaven, but also so that you can experience true peace while still here in this unpeaceful world—and because God loves you.

Genesis 8:5-19

After the great flood, the waters finally receded. While Noah was waiting, he sent out a raven and it flew here and there. Then he sent out a dove, but with no place for it to land, it returned to him. He waited seven days then sent the dove out again. It returned with a freshly picked olive leaf, so Noah knew that the water had gone down. He waited another seven days then sent the dove out again. This time, it didn't return so Noah knew the water had dried up, but did he leave the ark? No. He waited.

I wonder if Noah felt the warm and fuzzies for his family during their shut in. When we get to chapter nine, we will learn that life in Noah's family was not quite so perfect, so why did he wait to leave the ark? He was waiting on God. It seems that Noah actually waited for nearly two more months before God finally told him that it was time to come out.

Why did he wait for God's instruction? Why didn't he just burst outside the doors of the ark and run and jump on the dry land? His faith must have made him a patient man. Noah was pleasing to God, so Noah must have had a good understanding of Him. His faith helped him to wait for the One who could see all, the One who knew all. Noah's safety depended on listening for God's instruction. If only we could find a way to be still long enough to listen for

God's voice, He might just give us the wisdom to make the right choices. God will never lead you to destruction.

So how do you get answers from God? Start by asking Him questions. Pick up your Bible. Put your phone down. Talk to Him as you curl up to go to sleep. Then just listen. Ask and ye shall receive. I'm not going to promise you that all answers come right away. They don't. They won't come until God knows you're ready to hear them.

Genesis 8:20-9:17

The first thing that Noah did when he left the ark was build an altar to the Lord. He took of every clean animal and offered burnt offerings to God. The Lord smelled the soothing aroma and said that He would never again destroy every living thing. God was faithful to Noah, and Noah was faithful to God.

God blessed Noah and his sons and told them to be fruitful and multiply. He gave man charge over the animals and said that they shall be meat for them, just as the plants. His only stipulation was not to eat the blood. God requires the lifeblood for Himself just as He requires the life of every man.

God also said that whomever sheds the blood of man, by man shall his blood be shed. This is scriptural justification for supporting capital punishment. This is why so many Christians don't take issue with the death penalty. What's crazy though is that the same people who are against the death penalty are usually in favor of abortion. Allowing evil to live while killing the innocent is just plain backwards. As it will be in the end, what's good will be bad; what's bad will be good.

According to 2nd Timothy 3:1-5, in the last days, people will not love what's good. They will be lovers of self and money. They will be proud, arrogant, abusive, disobedient, ungrateful, unholy, heartless, unappeased, slanderous, without self-control, brutal. Watch the news lately?

Isaiah 5:20 *Woe unto them who call evil good, and good evil; who substitute darkness for light, and light for darkness...*

God gave the world another chance with Noah and his family, and He made them a promise. He promised to never destroy the earth by flood again. As part of his covenant with Noah, his future generations, and all living things, He placed a token in the clouds as a reminder of that promise. The token is the rainbow.

What's good will be bad; what's bad will be good.

Genesis 9:18-29

The three sons of Noah were Shem, Ham, and Japheth. They were all blessed by God. Ham apparently was the troublemaker, the black sheep of the family. He embarrassed and humiliated his father, and in return, Noah cursed Ham's son Canaan. Ouch. Noah was found righteous by God, but Noah wasn't perfect and neither was his son.

What did Ham do? Well, Noah planted a vineyard and then got drunk on his own wine. Oops. He probably shouldn't have done that because then he uncovered himself, and his son Ham walked in on him, saw him naked, and instead of covering him up, he ran off to tell his brothers. His two brothers, however, found a way to cover up their father without looking at him. They showed respect to their father, but Ham didn't. Because of Ham's actions, Noah put a curse on his son Canaan. The curse upon Canaan meant that he and his descendants would be a servant to Ham's brothers for generations to come. That curse came true.

9:25-27 *Cursed be Canaan; a servant of servants shall he be unto his brethren. Blessed be the Lord God of Shem; and Canaan shall be his servant. God shall enlarge Japheth, and he shall dwell in the tents of Shem; and Canaan shall be his servant.*

Was Noah overreacting? That probably depends on how much was left out of the story. We are only told the basics in scripture. Some Bible scholars, however, believe that "seeing nakedness" in the Bible might mean a little more than what it literally says. I'll let you use your imagination here. Whether literal or euphemistic, according to Leviticus 20:17, seeing the nakedness of a family member is wicked, and *he that does it shall bear his iniquity.*

Either way, Noah was one angry dad, and he cursed Ham's son Canaan. I wonder how Noah had the power to curse, but this curse actually came true, for Canaan's descendants were in fact servants to the descendants of Shem and Japheth. So was it the power of Noah that procured the curse? Or did God step in and answer Noah's strange request? Or was Noah's curse just a prophesy that God had put into his mind?

Canaan truly was cursed. His descendants were the servants of the descendants of Shem and Japheth. The Canaanites were also sexually perverse and worshipped strange idols. Later, God orders the Israelites to invade and completely destroy Canaan *that they teach you not to do after all their abominations...* (Deut. 20:18).

Noah lived 350 years after the flood, 950 years in all, probably long enough to see his curse upon Ham's descendants take shape. And you thought your family was dysfunctional!

GENESIS 10-12

Genesis 10 & 11:9

The generations of the sons of Noah and The Tower of Babel:

The sons of Japheth and their sons settled on the shores of the Black and Caspian Seas. Some Biblical scholars believe this is modern-day Turkey.

The sons of Ham and their sons established Babel, Nineveh, Canaan, Sodom and Gomorrah, and others. These places did not have the best of reputations, so it seems the curse of Ham did continue on. They settled along the Mediterranean coast.

The sons of Shem and their sons eventually went on down the line to Abram, who later became Abraham. This is the line from which Jesus came. They settled north of the Persian Gulf.

Originally, the whole earth spoke the same language. The descendants of Noah traveled east and eventually settled in the land of Shinar (ancient Babylonia). They made bricks and mortar and built themselves a city and a tower whose height would reach the heavens. They wanted to make a name for themselves and attract settlers like moths to a flame. This was in direct opposition to what God had told them to do: *Be fruitful and multiply and go and fill the earth.*

The Lord came down to see the city and the tower that they had built. He was not pleased with their progressive nature, basically saying that if they could do this together, there's no telling what else they could do. But of course, He's God, and He knew exactly what they could do. Many Bible scholars believe they used this tower to worship other gods. The people called their tower "Gate of God". We refer to it as the Tower of Babel. The term "babel" is linked to a Hebrew word meaning "to confuse".

God confused their language so they couldn't work together anymore. After all, they were working together to defy Him. In order to proceed with His original plan, He scattered them all about the earth, in effect creating all the different cultures of the world. This was His plan. He will have His victory.

How does this relate to modern times? When you get too many smart people in a room, innovative ideas evolve. Unfortunately, they are not always created for the good of God's people. Smart phones, for instance, are amazing contraptions, but in many ways are inherently bad. Could these be our modern day towers of Babel?

God knocked down their tower. I expect He will take care of ours too.

Genesis 11:10-12:3

Hundreds of years and nine generations passed from Shem (son of Noah) to Abram. In fact, Shem was still alive and kickin' when Abram was born, and if I did my math correctly, they were actually both alive at the same time for 110 years.

Terah came from the line of Shem. He was the father of Abram, Nahor, and Haran. Haran was the father of Lot and Milcah. He died in the land of Ur. Abram married Sarai, and Nahor married Milcah. They all left Ur, and headed toward the land of Canaan, but instead stopped and settled in Haran where Terah died at the age of 205. God told Abram to move on (to Canaan). There God would make him a great nation. He would bless him and make his name great so that he would be a blessing.

Abram's name would be great, and God wanted him to use his great name in order to be a BLESSING. That's interesting. Are today's famous folks a blessing? Well, maybe some of them, sometimes. Occasionally, we see them on T.V. as spokespersons for good and important endeavors, but other times we see them touting abortion and bashing people who don't agree with their views. Unfortunately, many celebrities don't use their name as a blessing, but as a curse, luring others into a trap of selfishness and sin, dragging them along into darkness.

God also promised Abram that He would bless those who bless him, and He would curse those who curse him, and that in him all the families of the earth would be blessed. This last promise was fulfilled through the line of Abram when Jesus was born and died for our sins.

Jesus just might be the most famous man who ever lived. He endorsed the protection of children and widows, mercy and compassion for others, repentance of sin, and forgiveness. He did not endorse tolerance, especially tolerance of sin. He did not endorse loving self above others, but instead wanted us to help each other, to love thy neighbor as thyself, to lay down our own lives for our friends.

Jesus has used His great name as a blessing. His fame has endured for over 2000 years, not come and gone with a generation of fans. He is God's Son. He came to this earth to sacrifice Himself for you so that you wouldn't have to suffer eternally for your own dark deeds. He painfully took your punishment upon Himself. No one deserves His mercy, yet He offers it freely, pleading with you to accept it, because He knows if you don't, you're lost forever, and that my friends, not only breaks His heart, but mine also.

Genesis 12:4-20

At age seventy-five, Abram took his wife Sarai and his nephew Lot and went into Canaan. The Lord appeared to Abram and said *To your descendants I will give this land.* With gratitude, Abram built an altar to the Lord in the same place He had appeared to him. Abram proceeded on and built another altar to the Lord by the mountain.

Since there was famine in the land, Abram and Sarai went into Egypt. Before they arrived, Abram told his wife to say that she was his sister. She was very beautiful, and he was afraid that they would kill him and take her. In fact, Pharaoh's officials saw her beauty and took her to Pharaoh who took her as his own wife.

Because Pharaoh thought Sarai was Abram's sister, he treated him well and even gave him livestock, but the Lord struck Pharaoh and his house with plagues because of Sarai. When Pharaoh figured out what was going on, he gave Sarai back to Abram and ordered them to leave the land. He did not want the wrath of God to come down on him.

What was Abram thinking? What a foolish idea! He should have just trusted God in the first place. It's amazing to me how God has anointed imperfect men to be such important leaders. Noah got drunk and cursed his own family, Abram lied and gave up his wife to avoid his own demise, and well, most of us know all about King David (one of God's favorites), and King Solomon. If you don't, just wait! They were definitely men behaving badly. No, God does not choose leaders based on their purity. I imagine He chooses them based on their strengths, their belief in Him, and their ability to be the right man for the job.

The good Lord knows that our leaders are not blameless. I'm sure He shakes His head in astonishment at the things that come out of their mouths and the sins they commit. It's easy to bash them, but that doesn't really do any good, does it? Instead let's pray for them—all of them. Lord knows they need it!

GENESIS 13-20

Genesis 13 & 14

Abram left Egypt with his wife, his nephew Lot, and all of their livestock, silver, and gold. He went back to the place where he had built an altar then called on the name of the Lord. Lot also had livestock, so much that the land could not sustain them both, so he and Abram decided to split up with Abram settling in the land of Canaan, while Lot chose for himself all the valley of the Jordan, moving his tents as far as Sodom. The men of Sodom were exceedingly wicked, but Lot remained righteous.

God told Abram that the land lying north, south, east, and west of where he stood would be his and his descendants' forever. God promised Abram that He would make his descendants as the dust of the earth, meaning they would be great in numbers.

After a few years, there was rebellion and war among the kingdoms—four kings against five. The kings of Sodom and Gomorrah fled and fell into the tar pits of the valley of Siddim. Those who survived fled to the hill country taking all the food supply and goods of Sodom and Gomorrah. To their detriment, they also took Abram's nephew with them. When Abram heard, he took his trained men, over 300 by that time, and set out to find Lot. He pursued them, defeated them, and brought back all they had taken, including his nephew.

After his return, the king of Sodom went to meet Abram at the valley of Shaveh (the King's Valley). Melchizedek, king of Salem and a priest of God, brought out bread and wine and blessed Abram. In return, Abram gave him a tenth of all the spoils of war. The king of Sodom told Abram to give the people to him but to keep all the goods for himself. He rejected the king's offer, refusing to be obligated to anyone but God. In the end, Abram took only his own men and the food they had already eaten, but he did allow his allies to take the spoils due them. Abram wanted there to be no mistake that his loyalty was to God alone, and that he was not to be under the debt of the king.

To whom do we owe our allegiance? Our country? Our president? Our laws? Though Jesus does tell us in Mark 12:17 to render unto Caesar what is Caesar's (pay our taxes), our true allegiance should belong to God and His Word. Just because some of the laws in our country allow things that are an abomination to God, does not mean we are to partake. Though we are expected to follow the law of the land, we are to be separate from our faithless society and choose God's will over our own. That's not always easy considering that social media, news networks, movies, TV shows, video games, and even some churches brainwash people into tolerating sin. God understands the battle, but He also expects us to stand strong, promising that He will not only stand with us, but in front of us.

Genesis 15

Abram had a vision in which God told him to fear not, that he would receive a great reward. Abram questioned God about the fact that he was still childless, and God assured him he would have his own biological child who would be his heir, that his descendants would be like the stars, innumerable. Abram believed Him, but then turned around and questioned Him, asking for a sign.

A deep sleep fell onto Abram in a horror of great darkness. The Lord told him with surety his seed would be a stranger in a land that is not theirs. They would be servants afflicted for four-hundred years, but the nation in which they serve would be judged by God. Afterward, his descendants would come out with great substance, and Abram would live to a very old age, and in the fourth generation, his descendants would come again to the land God promised Abram.

During those four-hundred years, the Amorite (meaning all the Canaanite tribes) would continue in their iniquity in that promised land until the Israelites returned to destroy them. God made a covenant with Abram that day, that unto his seed He has designated for them the land from the river of Egypt unto the great river Euphrates, though other tribes will occupy it until it is returned to God' chosen people.

The prophecy given to Abram by God was about the Israelites who were slaves in Egypt for four-hundred years until Moses led them to the promised land. Before Abram had any children, God kept promising him that his descendants would be many, but years would go by before God gave him a child. It can be difficult to keep the faith when it takes years for our prayers to be answered, but even though he was impatient, Abram believed God, and boy did God deliver!

Genesis 16

God had been promising an heir for Abram and Sarai, but as usual, God was on His timing, not theirs. To this point, Sarai had been unable to bear children, so she had this horrible idea to allow Abram to impregnate her Egyptian maid Hagar. Maybe Abram had faith in God, but his wife was tired of waiting and decided to take matters into her own hands. That was a mistake we are all still paying for today. It's also another biblical example of the wife leading the husband astray, again with the husband easily going along with it putting up little fight. (Remember Adam and Eve?) No wonder God had the idea for wives to obey their husbands. The wives got into too much trouble on their own!

Abram agreed to this plan, though he should have known better too. After ten years of living in Canaan, Abram slept with Hagar and she conceived. This was Sarai's plan, but it came back to bite her because now Hagar despised her. Sarai blamed Abram, and he told her to deal with Hagar whichever way she pleased. Sarai treated Hagar harshly causing her to flee. However, an angel of the Lord found Hagar and told her to go back and submit to Sarai's authority. Moreover, the angel told her that he would greatly multiply her descendants, and that because the Lord had seen her affliction, she would bear a son whom would be named Ishmael. (Ishmael means "God hears".) Hagar was astonished and called out to the name of the Lord. She did bear 86-year-old Abram a son, and Abram called him Ishmael.

Unfortunately, Ishmael would turn out to be a *wild donkey of a man whose hand would be against everyone, and everyone's hand would be against him.* He would live to the east of all his brothers. This could be literal but also figurative as the descendants of Ishmael have remained in conflict with the descendants of Isaac (Abram and Sarai's promised son who would come thirteen years after Ishmael). In fact, Ishmael is recognized as a prophet of Islam and an ancestor of many Arab tribes who are still in conflict with Christians and Jews to this day.

Just as we are still suffering the consequences of Eve's sin who was kicked out of the Garden of Eden, we also still suffer the consequences of Sarai's sin by living in conflict with the descendants of Ishmael. Our only saving grace is

Jesus Christ who died on that cross for us, who paid for our sins, who took our punishment on Himself so that we wouldn't have to face a horrifying eternity without God.

What's the take-away here? Eve and Sarai decided to control their own lives instead of trusting God. How did that work out for them? How did that work out for us thousands of years later? Not so good, right? How many generations will have to pay for our own impatience with God? Let's learn a lesson from their mistakes. As difficult as it is to wait, trust God's timing. He sees the whole moving picture while we only see a still frame.

Genesis 17

In chapter 17, Abram is 99 years old. God tells him to *walk before Me and be blameless,* and establishes a covenant with him—that He would multiply him exceedingly. Abram didn't say, *Yeah, yeah. I've heard it all before.* No. Abram fell on his face before God, and never lost faith that God would carry through with His promises.

God changed Abram's name to Abraham, meaning "father of many". He also promised him success and said that kings would come forth from him, and He extended that promise to Abraham's descendants, to be their God and to give them all the land of Canaan as their everlasting possession. However, God also ordered him to keep His covenant, him and his generations to come. God required that every male among them be circumcised, and every male baby be circumcised at eight days old. Any male who was not circumcised would be cut off from His people.

As for Sarai, God changed her name to Sarah. He said He would bless her and give her a son, that she would be the mother of nations. Upon hearing this, Abraham fell down and laughed. After all, he was pushing 100, and Sarah was 90. I doubt that God found that amusing, but you never know. God does have a sense of humor. Just look at the giraffe! As for Ishmael, God promised to bless him and multiply him exceedingly, that he would become the father of 12 princes and a great nation, but His covenant was with Abraham's descendants through Isaac, his son with Sarah, and not Ishmael.

After God finished speaking with Abraham, Abraham took Ishmael and all of his male servants and circumcised them, just as he was told. He was 99 years old. Ishmael was 13. Abraham's circumcision, especially at his age, proved his faith in God. God asked Abraham to do many difficult things in his life, things that most of us would not be able to do. Each time, Abraham's faith was proven, and God rewarded him greatly.

Obviously, Abraham was not a perfect man. He was not without sin, but God loved him and made him the father of many nations. Our God is good and loves us regardless of our sinful nature, and He uses even the least perfect of men to His glory.

Genesis 18

One hot sunny day, Abraham was hanging out in front of his tent when the Lord appeared to him. He looked up and saw three men. (God in human form plus two angels.) He ran to meet them and bowed himself to the earth. He then scurried around to bring them food to eat and water to wash their feet. They asked after Sarah who was in the tent. The Lord told Abraham that by the next year, his wife would surely have a son. Sarah overheard this and laughed because of her old age. God asked Abraham, *Why does Sarah laugh? Does she think it too difficult a task for the Lord?* Sarah denied laughing, but He had caught her in the act. God again promised that she would have a son by the next year.

God had chosen Abraham to raise his children to keep the way of the Lord by doing righteousness and justice, and He hesitated in telling Abraham why He was there and what He was about to do (destroy the city), but the outcry of Sodom and Gomorrah was great and their sin was exceedingly grave. The men rose up and walked with Abraham toward Sodom. Abraham asked God if He would really wipe away the righteous with the wicked. Abraham haggled with God until God said that if he could find ten righteous people within the city, He would not destroy it. God then departed, and Abraham returned to his place.

If you grew up in Sunday School, then you already know the outcome of this story. Abraham did not find ten righteous people in all of Sodom and Gomorrah, and God did destroy the city.

There are still many righteous people in our country, but there are fewer and fewer with each generation as they distance themselves from God. Will He destroy our country too someday? The book of Revelation discusses the kingdoms that will fight each other in the end. Our country is not mentioned. There are different theories as to the reason for that, regardless, it should give us pause.

Genesis 19

The two angels that had been visiting with Abraham and the Lord went into Sodom. Abraham's nephew, Lot, was sitting at the gate when they entered. He rose to meet them and invited them to stay at his home. That night the men of the city surrounded the house and demanded that Lot's two guests (the angels) come out. Their plan was to have immoral relations with them. Lot went outside and begged the men of his community not to act wickedly. He even offered to send out his two daughters. (This is one of those moments in the Bible where you stop and say WHAT?)

Yep, he was actually willing to let these men attack his own daughters in order to protect the two angels. I don't understand it either, but it's right there in the Bible. This is another reminder that God uses imperfect people to carry out His will. Anyway, the two angels grabbed Lot and dragged him inside and shut the door. They then struck the wicked men with blindness.

The angels told Lot to gather his family and leave, for the Lord had sent them to destroy the city. Lot's future sons-in-law did not believe him, and they wouldn't leave. When morning came, the angels took Lot, his wife, and two daughters and helped them escape the city. They told Lot to go to the mountains and warned them not to look back or they would be swept away. Lot begged the angels to instead allow them to escape to the town of Zoar. They granted his request and promised not to destroy it. The next morning, with Lot and his family in a safe place, the Lord rained down fire and brimstone on Sodom and Gomorrah. He overthrew those cities and the valley and all their inhabitants. Lot's wife did what she was told not to do—she looked back, and she turned into a pillar of salt.

Lot was still afraid, so he took his two daughters to the mountains to live in a cave. His daughters were worried that there were no men to be found to carry on the family line, so they devised a plan to get their father drunk and seduce him in order to become pregnant. Gross, right? Lot did not know what they had done. The elder daughter bore a son named Moab who became the father of the pagan Moabites who lived east of the Dead Sea, and the younger daughter bore a son named Ben-ammi who became the father of the sons of Ammon (the pagan Ammonites) who lived northeast of the Dead Sea.

What's our lesson from this chapter? Though God is love, eventually He runs out of patience.

Genesis 20

We've heard it said that history repeats itself. Well, only twenty chapters into the first book of the bible, Abraham is already repeating his mistakes. Remember back in Genesis 12 when Abraham told his wife to say she was his sister so that the Egyptians wouldn't kill him and take her (they would just take her instead)? Well, Abraham is up to his old tricks.

Abraham and Sarah go into Gerar. He once again tells Sarah to say she is his sister. His reasoning is that being an ungodly place, they will surely kill him to take his beautiful wife. I can just imagine Sarah sighing to herself and questioning that vow to obey her husband, but obey she did, and Abimelech, king of Gerar did take her.

Technically, Abraham did not lie. Sarah was in fact Abraham's father's daughter. I assume they were half siblings. Marrying a blood relative was acceptable in many cultures back then, but God later changed that practice through the law of Moses by strictly forbidding it (Leviticus 18).

God had a little discussion with Abimelech in a dream, that he was a dead man for taking Sarah. He claimed ignorance of her marriage and promised he had not touched her. God assured him that He knew, that He Himself had kept him from Sarah. God had intervened and kept Abimelech from sinning, arranging things in such a way that he either never had the chance, or he lacked desire for her. I wish it were that easy for us. I wish God would keep us from sinning, but He gives us free will. In this case, I'm guessing that God did not want Sarah to be defiled, as she was about to become the mother of all nations.

God does promise to provide a way out for those who are about to sin. He puts up roadblocks to keep us from our sinful goals, but we are often so determined that we bulldoze straight through those roadblocks in order to have our own way. It's only in hindsight that we realize God had provided a way out, just for us to ignore it.

God warned Abimelech to release Sarah back to Abraham or death would follow. In fact, God had already taken action against him by closing the wombs of his household. Abimelech gave Sarah back along with gifts of silver, oxen, sheep, and servants, and he told Abraham he could settle wherever he pleased. Abraham then prayed to God, and Abimelech and his household were healed from God's judgement.

I hope Abraham finally learned from this (the second time around). His sin ended up hurting Abimelech and his household, not Abraham. Sometimes life is unfair. It seems the sinner is rewarded while those affected by the sin are the ones to suffer. I don't know how Abraham felt, but I could guess that Sarah had plenty to say about it, and that might have been punishment enough. I wonder if they had doghouses back then.

GENESIS 21-25

Genesis 21:1-8

God finally fulfilled a long-awaited promise to Sarah. In their old age, she conceived and bore Abraham a son, in God's own appointed time. This son was Isaac, whose name means laughter. Abraham circumcised him at eight days old, as God had commanded.

Sometimes it's hard to wait on God's timing. Sarah was too old to have babies, yet God provided. She even lost her faith and pushed her husband on her maid so that he could have a son, yet God still provided. When God makes a promise, He keeps it. Patience may be a virtue, but even God's children are lacking. In a world of immediate gratification, patience is not something we have mastered. But God is still in control, and He never defaults.

We are all waiting for something in our lives. Some of us sit around and impatiently grumble. Some of us work toward our goals (also impatiently), but God will provide in His timing, not ours. Right now He's laying out all the pieces of our story to fit together perfectly. If we think about it,

God's plans are always better than our own. What's that saying? Man makes plans and God laughs.

Genesis 21:9-21

Abraham's Sarah was finally given a son, the son God had long-promised. Her happiness knew no bounds until jealousy reared its ugly head when Ishmael (Abraham's son with Hagar), was caught mocking Sarah and her new child. As a result, Sarah demanded Abraham to send Hagar and Ishmael away.

Abraham was hesitant—after all, Ishmael was his son, but God told him to do it, promising He would make a nation of Ishmael, which He did, but Isaac was to be the special one. Isaac was the prophesied son through which Abraham's descendants would be named. A distressed Abraham did as he was told and sent them away.

Hagar and Ishmael left and wandered about in the wilderness of Beersheba until they ran out of water, but God heard their cries and provided a well. God stayed with Ishmael as he grew up in the wilderness of Paran where he became an archer and later married a woman from Egypt. Though Ishmael's existence was a result of the sin of Abraham and Sarah's lack of faith, God was still with him. God still had compassion for him and Hagar.

Throughout the Bible God shows compassion for His children when they fall short, but what about unbelievers? Does He have compassion for them? We know that God intervenes on His children's behalf, but an unbeliever rejects God's help, doesn't he? We know that we can't help people who don't want our help, but God can do anything.

Maybe He helps unbelievers through the prayers of the righteous. If we continue to pray for the lost, maybe God will answer our prayers. So, don't give up on lost loved ones. God loves us all, and it is not His desire to see anyone perish, but for all to come to Him and have everlasting life in Heaven.

Genesis 21:22-34

While Hagar and Ishmael were wandering in the wilderness of Beersheba, Abraham and King Abimelech were having their own squabbles over a well. Apparently, unbeknownst to him, Abimelech's men had seized Abraham's well. They worked out their differences, however, and made a covenant with each other at Beersheeba. Abraham planted a Tamarisk tree to mark the spot and then called on the name of the Lord.

Abraham often called on the name of the Lord. Obviously he wasn't perfect, but God sought him out and made him a great leader. Abraham was a sinner, just like Adam, just like Eve, just like Sarah, Hagar, and Ishmael, but God was with them all and chose Abraham to be the father of many nations, in spite of his imperfections.

Genesis 22:1-24 The Ultimate Sacrifice

What would you give up for God? Would you give up your favorite sin? Would you give up your family? Would you even give up Sundays? Most of us are too weak to give up any of these, even Sundays.

There once came a day when God asked Abraham to give up the most precious thing in his life. God had promised that Isaac would be special, but it seemed He had changed the plan. He instead asked Abraham to sacrifice his beloved son, the most important thing in his life. Not only did God ask Abraham to give up Isaac, He asked for Abraham to perform the sacrifice himself. Would you be able to fulfill that request? I wouldn't.

God asked Abraham to take Isaac, whom God knew he loved, to one of the mountains in the land of Moriah and offer him there as a burnt offering. Abraham even split the wood himself for the offering. They traveled until the third day when they came to the mountain. Abraham took the wood, the fire, the knife, and Isaac who believed they were going there to worship. Isaac questioned his father about the lamb they were to sacrifice. Abraham answered that God would provide the lamb.

I wonder how Abraham felt as he prepared the fire that was to consume his precious son. I wonder how he felt as he bound him and placed him on that altar. I wonder how he felt as he took the knife and pulled his arm back to slay his beloved child. I wonder at the relief he must have felt when the angel of the Lord stopped him in his tracks and told him not to harm the boy. God, in all His glory, instead provided a ram for the sacrifice.

Abraham named the place "The Lord will provide." God had tested his faith, his fear, his loyalty, and he passed the test. Would we? Notice that God asked Abraham to do it, not Sarah. Maybe God knew that a mother's heart could never willingly give up her child, maybe not even for God. As a mother I would gladly sacrifice my own life for my son, but I don't think I could ever sacrifice his.

On that great day, not only did the Lord provide, He rewarded Abraham with the promise that He would greatly bless him and his seed which He would multiply as the stars of heaven and the sand on the seashore. I bet if you look back on your pitfalls, you will see that the Lord provided for you also.

I truly hope God never puts me to Abraham's test. I would fail. Sometimes we feel tested and tried over and over again by God, and we are constantly proven weak, but no test compares to that of giving up your child. So, the next time we grumble about giving up our sin or our Sundays, just remember Abraham and what he was asked to give up, and remember what God sacrificed for us—His only Son, Whom He loved. We are lucky. God has been easy on us after all.

Genesis 23

Sarah lived to be 127 years old then died in the land of Canaan where Abraham mourned and wept for her. He was a stranger in the land and needed a burial site for his wife, so he asked the sons of Heth for help. They wanted to give him one of their sepulchers, but he wanted Ephron the Hittite to sell him the cave of Machpelah which resided at the end of Ephron's field.

Abraham spoke to Ephron in front of the people of the land. Ephron wanted to give the cave to Abraham, but he rejected the gift and insisted on paying for it for its worth. Abraham paid 400 shekels of silver to Ephron for the cave and its surrounding land, and he made sure of the boundary lines with the people as his witness.

This was to be the location where he would bury his beloved. He wanted it secure. He paid a fair price for the field and the cave, and he did it in front of many witnesses. He could have accepted it as a free gift, but he didn't. Abraham was no dummy.

In the old days, there was a time when people were too prideful to owe anyone a debt. Now, we are all in debt up to our ears. We think nothing of getting a loan for our homes, our cars, our vacations. We have no pride when it comes to borrowing. It's true that we are in different times. Everything costs too much now to be able to save for it before we purchase, but doesn't it feel good when our debts are finally paid off? I hate paying interest, not that I have much choice, but when I add it all up, I cringe. Therefore, I always try to pay more than that minimum payment. I always try to get things paid off as soon as I am able, and what a relief it is when that debt is paid.

God expects us to pay our debts and live within our means (yes, I know that's difficult). He blesses us with extra so that we can help others, not so that we can help ourselves to all the extra goodies of life. I must admit I'm a little bit of a hypocrite on this subject. I like the extras too, but nothing feels better than to help someone out, tip someone a little (or a lot) extra when they are working hard, send money to Wounded Warriors or Shriner's Hospital for Kids or St. Jude's. It is expected when God blesses us—not to reward the lazy, but to help those who cannot always help themselves.

Genesis 24

Here's your sign...

Abraham was getting along in age, and after the death of his wife Sarah, he wanted to secure a proper wife for his son Isaac. Unfortunately, they lived among the Canaanites, who were worshippers of idols and lived outside the covenant of God, so he decided to send his servant to his homeland to pursue this wife.

Abraham chose his oldest and most trusted servant to complete this task. He instructed him to go to his former country, to his relatives, to look for a wife for Isaac. He also forbade Isaac from going with him. Why would he forbid Isaac from going with him? Well, Abraham had been promised by God that the Canaanite land would be given to his descendants, so it was important that his descendants remain there. Perhaps he was afraid his son might not return if allowed to go back to the old country.

The servant was apprehensive and questioned his own ability to convince the right woman to return to Canaan with him. Abraham assured him that the Lord would send an angel ahead of him and that he indeed would take a wife for his son from there.

Before the servant entered the city of Nahor (Abraham's brother), he paused by the well at evening time when the women would go out to draw water. He prayed to God for a sign that whichever woman offered him water and also offered to water his camels, she would be the one the Lord had chosen for Isaac. Behold, along comes beautiful Rebekah, granddaughter of Abraham's brother, who incidentally fulfills that sign.

Rebekah takes the servant home with her to her family where he explains the whole story. Rebekah was willing to go to Isaac; her family was willing to allow it. When they reached Isaac, the servant explained Abraham's plans. Isaac loved Rebekah, and she was a comfort to him after the loss of his mother Sarah.

Have you ever asked for a sign from God? Have you ever noticed those pesky little red flags that seem to be a warning? God guides us all the time. We just have to pay attention.

For He will command His angels concerning you to guard you in all your ways. On their hands they will bear you up, lest you strike your foot against a stone. Psalm 91:11-12

Genesis 25

Don't be an Esau.

After Sarah's death, Abraham married Keturah. She bore him several more children whom he sent to live in the east, away from Isaac. Though he gave gifts to these children while still living, Isaac was the one to whom he left everything. Abraham lived to the ripe old age of 175 years, satisfied with his life. When he died, Isaac and Ishmael buried him with Sarah. It was after the death of Abraham that God blessed Isaac as He had promised.

Ishmael (Abraham's son by Hagar) had twelve sons, each having their own village named after them—12 princes according to their tribes. They settled east of Egypt, in defiance of their relatives. Ishmael lived to be 137 years old.

Isaac (Abraham's son by Sarah) married Rebekah who had troubled conceiving. Isaac went to the Lord in prayer and she became pregnant with twins who struggled within her. God told Rebekah that two nations were in her womb—that two peoples would come from within her. One people would be stronger than the other, and the older would serve the younger. When Isaac was sixty years old, Rebekah gave birth to this set of twins. The first baby born was Esau, who was "red all over like a hairy garment." Then his brother was born holding onto the heel of Esau, so they named him Jacob.

Esau grew up to be a skillful hunter, but Jacob was a peaceful man. Isaac loved Esau, but Rebekah loved Jacob. This probably didn't help their relationship. One day, when Esau came in from the field famished, he found Jacob cooking stew. Jacob offered Esau a deal: that he would give him a bowl of stew in trade for Esau's birthright. As the oldest brother, Esau was to receive the birthright, not Jacob, but he easily gave it all up for some food. Remember God had promised Abraham that Isaac would be blessed. Esau should have inherited that blessing but he easily gave it up.

Who was wrong in this scenario? Was Jacob wrong? Did he trick Esau? Or was Esau so unimpressed with God's blessing that he flippantly dismissed it? Verse 34 tells us that Esau despised his birthright. Malachi 1:2-3 states that God loved Jacob and loathed Esau. Therefore, Jacob and his descendants (the Israelites) were God's chosen people, and Esau's descendants, known as the Edomites (Genesis 36:43), were in conflict with them.

Like Esau, people flippantly reject God. Because of that, they cannot receive His blessings. I don't know about you, but I will take all the blessings God is willing to bestow on me, especially the blessing of going to Heaven someday.

GENESIS 26-28

Genesis 26:1-11

Like Father Like Son

A famine in the land forced Isaac to head to Gerar. The Lord appeared to him and told him to sojourn in this land (temporarily) and he would receive the blessing promised to Abraham. God would give Isaac his own land, and by his descendants all the nations of the earth would be blessed. Why? Because Abraham had obeyed God, Isaac would reap the blessings. Isaac lived in Gerar, but he was only supposed to stay temporarily. He didn't listen to God and ended up in trouble.

Unfortunately, like father like son, Isaac told the citizens that his wife Rebekah was his sister, for the same reasons Abraham had lied about Sarah (Genesis 12:13). They were pretty, and their husbands feared they would be killed for their wives, but Abimelech, king of the Philistines, figured out the truth and became angry with Isaac for lying. After all, what if one of the men had lain with Rebekah? It would have brought guilt upon them, he said. Well, they would have been guilty anyway, but that's a king's logic for you. Isaac fessed up to the king and the king warned everyone not to touch Rebekah or Isaac.

Why was Abimelech so accommodating to Isaac? After all, Isaac had lied to him. But instead of punishing him, the king threatened the people saying, "He who touches this man or his wife shall surely be put to death."

Do you think he knew about the covenant between Abraham and God? Do you think he could see that Isaac was protected by God? Isaac didn't exactly rear up to him looking for a fight. Maybe it was Isaac's peaceful ways that prompted his mercy. Either way, Abimelech backed down, and Isaac was poised to inherit the blessings once promised to Abraham.

Isaac was blessed because his father obeyed God. What inheritance will we leave our children? Will they be blessed by our behavior? Or just the opposite?

Genesis 26:12-35

Peaceful Isaac

Isaac sowed in the land of Gerar and reaped the same year a hundredfold. The good Lord blessed him mightily, and Isaac became an extremely wealthy man. The Philistines grew jealous and filled up his ancestral water wells with dirt. Abimelech (the king) told Isaac to leave for he was afraid of Isaac's power. Isaac did leave, but he didn't go far, dwelling in the valley of Gerar. Isaac dug up the wells of Abraham, which had been filled by the Philistines after Abraham's death, and Isaac's servants dug in the valley, but the herdsmen of Gerar fought Isaac's servants over the well. There were many arguments over territorial rights, and each time Isaac peacefully moved on, digging another well and another well until finally no one contested him. Then he declared that the Lord had finally made room for them. Afterwards, he went to Beersheba where Abraham had also once dwelled.

The Lord appeared to Isaac and told him to fear not, that he would bless him and multiply his seed for Abraham's sake. And Isaac built an altar to the Lord right there. Then Abimelech showed up asking for an oath between them, for Abimelech knew that God was with Isaac. They made their oath of peace.

Esau (who was forty years old at the time) married Judith and Bashemath, who were both daughters of the Hittites. Isaac and Rebekah were not pleased.

Isaac seems to be a peaceful man. He trusted in God's promises, but though he was mightily blessed, he obviously did not lead an easy life. Someone was always waiting to agitate him, including his own son. Like Isaac, we have many blessings and many irritants. We can ask God why, or we can accept it and move on and continue to trust Him. After all, even God's favorites had their problems. Who are we to question ours?

Genesis 27 through 28:9

God Uses Bad for Good

Rebekah (wife of Isaac and mother of Jacob and Esau) forms a plan for Jacob to trick his father into giving him the blessing saved for his eldest son (Esau). Jacob goes along with it and steals his brother's blessings: heaven's dew, the earth's richness, an abundance of grain and new wine, lordship over his brothers and other nations, that those who curse him be cursed, and that those who bless him be blessed.

My first inclination after reading of this trickery was to be incensed at the injustice done to poor Esau. However, when I read a little more, then read a little back, I realized the reason this happened. Esau was just not fit for the blessing. Yes, Rebekah was deceitful. She's a little unlikeable to me at the moment, and Jacob was tricky too, but what were their motives? Selfishness? Perhaps. Or maybe God used something bad to bring about something good. After all, the nations that came through Jacob became Israel, God's blessed nation. The nations that came through Esau would live in hostility.

Look back to Chp. 25. The Lord had told Rebekah that the twins in her womb were two nations, two peoples who would be separated. One would be stronger, and the older would serve the younger. Esau was older. Also, Esau so willingly sold his birthright to Jacob for a bowl of stew.

Was he really that hungry, or did he despise his birthright as the scripture says? Esau is not innocent in this story.

In Chp. 26, Esau married two Hittite women. (The Hittites worshipped many gods). This grieved Rebekah and Isaac. So, Esau was no sweet smelling rose. Does that make it okay for Rebekah and Jacob to cook up a plan to steal his blessing? My opinion is no. However, it makes sense. Plus, God already knew this was coming (The older will serve the younger).

So, Jacob gets Esau's birthright and Esau's blessing from his father Isaac. What does Esau get? Isaac tells him that his dwelling will be away from the earth's richness, away from the dew of heaven above, that he will live by the sword and serve his brother, but that one day he would throw his (Jacob's) yoke from off his neck. What does that mean? Eventually, the nations through Esau separate in rebellion from the nations of Jacob. That comes later in the bible.

Back to the story, Esau is seriously mad at his brother, so Rebekah sends Jacob away with instructions to go find a proper wife. What does Esau do? Just for spite, he goes to Ishmael (remember him?) to obtain even more wives. Remember that God had told Ishmael that his offspring would live in hostility toward all their brothers. Esau's bloodline was tainted. It was important for Jacob's to remain pure, for his is the bloodline from which Jesus comes.

There are many instances in the bible in which God uses bad to create good. In our world, many bad things are happening, and we need to pray about them, but if you are a child of faith, you will be able to see the blessings that God can bring out of such things.

Genesis 28:10-22

Jacob's Ladder

Following his parents' instructions, Jacob headed out toward Haran in his journey for a proper wife, but the sun was setting so he stopped for the night. He lay on the ground and used a stone for a pillow. Then he had a dream, but not just any ordinary dream. This dream would change his life.

In Jacob's dream, a ladder reached from the earth all the way to the heavens, and the angels of the Lord were using this ladder to ascend and descend from one to the other. The Lord stood above and declared that He was the God of Abraham and of Isaac, promising the land on which Jacob lay would be given to him and his descendants.

God told Jacob that his descendants would be like the dust of the earth, spreading to the north, south, east, and west, and that in him and in his descendants all the families of the earth would be blessed (Jesus came through the line of Jacob). God also promised Jacob that He would be with him, that He would take care of him, and that He would bring him back to his land. God promised He would not leave him until fulfilling that promise.

Jacob woke up, but he knew this was no ordinary dream. He knew that God had been there with Him, but he was afraid. He felt like this place on which he stood was some kind of gate to heaven. Jacob took the stone (his pillow) and set it up as a pillar and poured oil on it and called it "Bethel", replacing its previous name "Luz". Jacob then made a vow that if God took care of him and provided for him, and returned him to his father's house safely, then he would commit himself to God and make that stone which he set up as a pillar God's house, and he would give God back a tenth of all God gave him. I guess that's where tithing comes from.

This was not a deal Jacob made with the Lord. This was the promise of the Lord, and Jacob recognized and accepted that promise. God promises us too that He will always be with us, no matter what may come. God doesn't promise that the road will be smooth. In fact, the bible assures us that we will have troubles in this life. The only trouble-free life will be the one that begins when this one ends...if we accept the promises of the Lord.

GENESIS 29 - 30:1-24

Genesis 29

Jacob went on his journey and met Rachel while she was tending her sheep. He fell for her instantly and asked her father, Laban, for her hand in marriage. They made a deal that Jacob would serve Laban for seven years, then he would be allowed to marry Rachel.

After seven years, the wedding ensued. Unbeknownst to Jacob, however, he was tricked into marrying Leah, Rachel's not-so-pretty older sister. Jacob was incensed, but Laban insisted that the eldest sister must marry first.

They struck another deal in which Jacob was allowed to also marry Rachel one week after his wedding to Leah. In return, he would serve Laban another seven years. So, Jacob married his beloved Rachel one week after marrying Leah, whom he did not love.

The Lord knew that poor Leah was unloved, so He gave her many children. Rachel, on the other hand, had not been able to conceive. Leah had four sons with Jacob: Reuben, Simeon, Levi, and Judah.

Genesis 30:1-24

Rachel was very jealous that Leah could bear Jacob children when she had not. Rachel threatened Jacob to give her children or she would die. Was she threatening suicide or just being dramatic? Either way, Jacob was angered by her outburst, claiming that he was not God. It wasn't his fault.

Because it seems that no one ever learns from the lessons of history, Rachel gave her maid, Bilhah, to Jacob to bear him a child. Bilhah bore Jacob a son named Dan. Bilhah conceived again and gave Jacob another son, Naphtali, but then she stopped conceiving, and she too gave her maid, Zilpah to Jacob who bore him two sons, Gad and Asher.

Leah ended up giving Jacob two more sons: Issachar and Zebulun, and then a daughter, Dinah.

Finally, God took pity on Rachel and opened her womb. She bore Jacob a son whom they called Joseph.

We've read this same story before when Sarah gave her maid to Abraham when she could not bear him children. Though God had promised her she would, she didn't have enough faith. Abraham had a son with Hagar (Sarah's maid) named Ishmael, and later God fulfilled His promise to Sarah who gave birth to Isaac. The descendants of these two continue to fight to this day. It seems when we stop waiting on God, when we decide to fix things ourselves, when we take matters into our own hands, we only mess things up, and not just for ourselves, but possibly for future generations.

Genesis 30:25-31:55

Genesis 30:25-31:55

The Lord Protects Us

After all these years, Jacob was still serving Laban (Rachel's father). Laban believed that Jacob brought him prosperity in that the Lord had blessed him on Jacob's account, and he didn't want to see him go. Jacob was ready to go home, however.

They struck a deal in which Jacob would pasture and take care of Laban's animals. In return, he would keep all the striped, spotted, and black goats and lambs as his wages. Laban tried to cheat him by separating and hiding the spotted animals so that Jacob's herd would be smaller. Meanwhile, as Jacob took care of Laban's animals, he took the strong animals and put poplar and almond and plane tree in their water to increase their fertility. He did not do this for the weaker animals. The white flocks belonging to Laban, in the care of Jacob, ended up giving birth to goats and sheep that were black, striped, and spotted. A deal's a deal, and though Laban tried to cheat Jacob, the

Lord turned things around and multiplied Jacob's herd. Of course, this made Laban's sons angry and they accused Jacob of stealing their father's animals. The Lord told Jacob it was time to leave. Jacob took his wives, his children, his livestock, and all that belonged to him and headed to his father, Isaac, in the land of Canaan. Unfortunately, before they left, Rachel stole her father's idols.

Laban pursued Jacob in his anger for seven days and finally caught up to him in Gilead. However, the Lord came to Laban in a dream and warned him not to hurt Jacob. Laban questioned Jacob, asking why he fled with no good-bye, then he accused him of stealing his idols. Jacob had no idea that Rachel had taken them, and Laban did not find them since Rachel was sitting on them on top of her camel, but his suspicions did not wane.

At this point, Jacob exploded on Laban, pointing out all the years he'd served him, all he'd done for him. Laban didn't see it his way, of course, but they made a deal not to harm one another, with God as their witness. Then early the next morning, Laban kissed his daughters and grandchildren good-bye and went home.

The Lord took care of Jacob when his enemies were trying to cheat him and do him harm. The Lord takes care of us too. Though bad things do happen to God's children sometimes, He is always with us, protecting our hearts and our peace of mind. Besides, imagine all that He has protected us from that we don't even know about.

GENESIS 32

Genesis 32

Jacob Wrestles with God

Jacob is now on his way home, finally. Imagine how nervous he must be since the last time he'd been there, he put one over on his brother Esau to obtain the birthright, and then he was forced to flee.

In his wisdom, he sent a messenger ahead to his brother Esau to let him know he would be coming home and bringing his many flocks and herds with him. Esau's response? I will meet him with four-hundred men. Mmmmm...this could either be the makings of a big welcome-home party or possibly a miniature civil war. Jacob's nervousness grew.

Jacob may not be a perfect man, but he was definitely no dummy. He devised a plan to break up his herds into two groups. He would send one group ahead to meet Esau, while the other half he would slow-walk there along with his family and himself. That way, if Esau attacked the first group, the rest would have time to escape.

In his fear, Jacob prayed. How often do we pray while we are in the fox hole only to forget God once we are saved? We need to worship Him while things are good and still praise Him when things get tough. Anyway, Jacob reminded God that He was the One who sent Jacob home and promised that he and his descendants would prosper. I think it's funny that we think we need to remind God of His promises, but I guess it's therapeutic for us. God is so patient with us, isn't He?

After praying, Jacob decided to gift Esau 500 of his animals. It's not a bad strategy. Maybe that will ease his anger a bit. In my opinion, this is an example of God speaking to us. Jacob prayed about his situation, then an idea struck him. This often happens. We talk to God, and He answers us by popping ideas into our minds. All ideas do not come from God, however, so we should test our plans against scripture, and then talk to God for peace of mind and spirit. It's a great way to make a tough decision.

Jacob sent his family ahead and spent some time alone. He probably needed to get his mind right before meeting his brother again after all these years. That night he wrestled with a man until daybreak. Now, this could have been a dream. It is said that the man he wrestled with was God, whose face no one is allowed to see. The man allowed Jacob to overtake him, for it was near daybreak, and maybe he didn't want Jacob to see his face.

Maybe Jacob just wrestled with God through his prayers. Do we often do that in our prayers? Question God, remind God of His promises, try to make deals with Him? Maybe this was the true wrestling, but there was physical evidence left behind for Jacob to know just how real this experience was. The man dislocated the socket of Jacob's thigh, leaving him with a limp and physical evidence of a spiritual awakening.

Jacob must have recognized this man as God, for he would not let him go until he gave him a blessing. So, God removed the name Jacob, which means heel-catcher, and renamed him Israel, for he had striven with God and men and yet prevailed. Jacob knew he had encountered God, for he named the place Penuel, the face of God.

GENESIS 33

Genesis 33

Jacob is heading home, and his brother Esau is heading to meet him with an army of men. Jacob had done his brother wrong and was understandably nervous to meet up with him again, so when he saw his brother coming with four-hundred men, he bowed down seven times and referred to himself as the servant of Esau. He must have been surprised when Esau ran up to him and gave him a great big hug! They had a huge family reunion and each wife and all the children bowed down as they were introduced to Esau.

We aren't told why, but Esau showed love and compassion towards Jacob even though Jacob had stolen his birthright. Yet God chose Jacob to receive the blessing. He chose Jacob to carry the bloodline of Jesus. God chooses imperfect people to carry out His plans. That makes perfect sense when you realize that we are all imperfect people just trying to make our way through a fallen world. There is no one perfect to fulfill God's plans, except for Jesus. Jesus, who was without sin, took our sin upon Him and received our punishment so we wouldn't have to. That's love. Therefore, though we are imperfect Christians, we are made perfect in Christ.

When we stand before God to be judged someday, Jesus will stand before us and cover our sins. We will appear spotless before our Lord because of Jesus. Jesus wasn't just a prophet. He wasn't just a cool dude who preached about love. He was so much more than that. He is the Son of God, and we don't stand a chance to appear innocent before a holy God without Jesus blocking all our sins. We need Jesus in order to live in Heaven with God. There is no other way.

Jacob tried to give Esau gifts, but Esau tried to refuse them. "I have enough," he said. The Lord had been good to him also. Both brothers undeserving, yet blessed by God. We are undeserving too, and God still blesses us, but there is one gift we'd better not reject, and that's the gift of salvation that Jesus gave to us all. Many are still rejecting it. Why?

Genesis 34

Genesis 34

In Genesis 31:3, God told Jacob "Return to the land of your fathers and to your relatives, and I will be with you." Jacob loved and respected God, but apparently he still liked to take matters into his own hands. Even though he'd told Esau that he would be along shortly, he thought it would be good to stop early and build a place for himself in Succoth. He stayed there for a long time and then bought land near Shechem, still neglecting to go all the way home to his relatives. There he set up an altar to the Lord and called it El Elohe Israel, but he still had not followed God's command.

Now Dinah, one of Jacob's daughters, went out into the land of Shechem without her brothers, for they were with the flocks in the field. She left her place of safety and went into a heathen land to visit the women there. When Shechem, son of Hamor the Hivite, the ruler of that area, saw Dinah, he wanted her for his own. He was instantly obsessed with her and he took her against her will and defiled her. He desperately wanted to marry her, so Hamor went to Jacob to ask for her hand.

Jacob was displeased but could do nothing until his sons returned from the field, and when they returned, they were seriously ticked off and set their minds for revenge. They tricked Hamor and his son into a deal in which all the men of their city would get circumcised in order to be able to intermarry with their people. This of course, did not make them worshippers of God, but they were willing to do so in order to marry into Jacob's family. Jacob's sons deceived them.

When three days had passed, and all the men of the city were in pain from the circumcisions, Jacob's sons, Simeon and Levi, went into the city and slaughtered them, and took their sister back home. The other brothers looted the city and took the women and children. Jacob was furious with them for bringing trouble on their family. He knew the Canaanites and Perizzites would come looking for them, but the young men held their own and did not regret their revenge.

The Old Testament shows us that God's people were no saints. They could even be a violent people, yet God still loved them. Now, if Jacob had initially done what God said by going back home to his relatives, none of this would have ever happened.

Isn't it better to follow God's word than to follow our own plans? God wants to protect us, and He wouldn't send us into danger. However, He also gave us the free will to put ourselves smack dab into the middle of a mess. God sees what lies up ahead. We don't. He knows what we should do, so we should listen, but how do we listen? How do we know which way God wants us to go? First, we read the Bible and follow His commandments. If it's against God's Word, it's the wrong choice. Then, have conversations with God about your plans. The choice that brings you peace is the one God approves. Always pray before a big decision—or even a little one.

GENESIS 35

Genesis 35

God gave Jacob a new order. He told him to pack up and move to Bethel and to make an altar there for the Lord. Jacob then ordered his family to get rid of all their foreign gods and purify themselves. So they gave Jacob all their idols and the rings in their ears and he hid them under the oak near Shechem. Throughout their journey, the Canaanites seemed to be having their own problems, so they did not pursue Jacob and his family. God protected them.

When Jacob came to Luz, he built an altar and called the place El-bethel because that was where God had first revealed Himself when Jacob so long ago had fled from his home after stealing Esau's birthright.

God appeared to Jacob and blessed him and changed his name to Israel. He also commanded him to be fruitful and multiply. Then God gave Jacob a list of promises:

A nation and a company of nations shall come from you.

Kings shall come forth from you.

The land which I gave to Abraham and Isaac, will I give to you and to your descendants.

Afterwards, Jacob set up a pillar of stone and poured out a drink offering and oil upon it and named this place where God had spoken to him "Bethel".

Why did God change Jacob's name? The name Jacob means heel catcher, supplanter, deceiver, someone who trips people, who causes them to stumble. It's not a great name. Jacob's actions had once reflected his name, so God gave him a better name, Israel, which means God's fighter, triumphant with God, or God perseveres. This is a more worthy name for the father of God's chosen people, the Israelites.

On their journey from Bethel to Ephrath (Bethlehem), Rachel went into labor and died as she was giving birth. She named her son Ben-oni (son of my sorrow) because she knew she was dying. However, Jacob renamed him Benjamin (son of honor). He would be the last child whom he had with the love of his life. Jacob set a pillar over her grave, then they settled for a while near the tower of Eder.

Reuben (Jacob's firstborn) had relations with Bilhah, his father's concubine. Jacob was displeased and this eventually led to Reuben losing his birthright. Jacob had twelve sons from Leah, Rachel, Bilhah (Rachel's maid), and Zilpah (Leah's maid). Yes, it seems he was quite busy.

The sons of Leah: Reuben, Simeon, Levi, Judah, Issachar, and Zebulun.

The sons of Rachel: Joseph and Benjamin

The sons of Bilhah: Dan and Naphtali

The sons of Zilpah: Gad and Asher

Jacob finally returned to his father Isaac who lived to the ripe old age of 180. Isaac died and was buried by his sons, Jacob and Esau.

GENESIS 36

Genesis 36

Esau, also referred to as Edom, married women from the land of Canaan. As you may recall, his parents were very distressed over this, for they were not of a Godly people. He married Adah, the daughter of Elon the Hittite, and Oholibamah, the daughter of Anah and the granddaughter of Zibeon the Hivite. He also married Basemath, the daughter of Ishmael. Remember that Ishmael was the son of Abraham and Hagar (his wife's maid).

Esau was not a parent-pleaser. First, he sold his birthright for a bowl of stew, then he married a bunch of heathen women. Jesus definitely did not come from his part of the family. Esau had children with each of his wives in the land of Canaan, then took his family to another land away from his brother because he and Jacob each had too much livestock to be able to live together. Esau ended up living in the hill country of Seir with his growing family. Some of his descendants became kings in Edom before any king reigned over the sons of Israel.

Genesis 37

Genesis 37

Jacob settled in Canaan. When his young son Joseph was seventeen, he was quite the tattletale, and he was Jacob's favorite. Jacob even gave him a "coat of many colors". His brothers were very jealous and really didn't like him. One night, Joseph had a dream about his brothers in which they would bow down to him. He made the mistake of telling them about it, which only increased their hatred. Then he had another dream in which his brothers and his parents would bow down to him. His brothers were furious; Jacob rebuked him, but he didn't dismiss his son's dream.

One day, while Joseph's brothers were out in the pasture tending the flocks, Jacob sent his son to check on them. When they saw him coming, they hatched a treacherous plan to murder him, but Reuben stepped in. He came up with his own plan to throw him into a pit, but not to kill him. He was planning to later secretly rescue his little brother. However, while Joseph was in the pit, Judah decided it would be best to sell his brother as a slave to the

Ishmaelites for twenty shekels of silver, for he really didn't want his little brother to die either. Then the Ishmaelites sold him in Egypt to Potiphar, the captain of Pharaoh's bodyguard.

When Reuben came back to rescue Joseph, he wasn't in the pit. He tore his garments and panicked. The brothers then took Joseph's coat of many colors and dipped it in goat's blood and tricked their father into thinking he was dead. Jacob tore his clothes and wore sackcloth in mourning, refusing to be comforted.

Joseph was just the bratty little brother, but now is headed his way to Egypt to work for the pharaoh. We will soon read that God is good to Joseph, however. God never left him, nor does He ever leave us (even when we're bratty).

GENESIS 38

Genesis 38

This chapter focuses on Judah, one of Jacob's sons by Leah. Judah is the tribe of the bloodline of Jesus. It was important for Jesus to come from a pure bloodline, but as you will see, though the blood may be pure, not everyone in Jesus's family tree is spotless.

Judah left his brothers and married the daughter of a Canaanite man. They had three sons: Er, Onan, and Shelah. Er married Tamar, but he was a wicked man, so God put him to death. As was the custom, Onan married his brother's widow, but he refused to have children with her, so God put him to death also. At this point, Judah was afraid that if his third son married Tamar, as was expected, Judah would lose him too, so he told her to remain a widow for a while.

After the death of Judah's wife, Tamar, who tired of being a widow, tricked her father-in-law into sleeping with her, and she became pregnant. One can only imagine the drama this must have created. When Judah found out his daughter-in-law was pregnant, he wanted her burned to death, but that was before he found out he was the father of her unborn child, which turned out to be twins named Perez and Zerah. Zerah tried to be born first, but Perez made way and became the first born. Jesus comes from the line of Perez.

Perfect bloodline, imperfect people. No one is truly righteous except Jesus himself, and God has always used flawed people to carry out his purposes. He would have to since we are all flawed. Why are we all flawed? We live in this world, and the prince of this world is Satan. None of us could escape without the sacrifice of Jesus to cover our sins. Without Jesus, we would belong to Satan. There are only two choices, my friend, and we can only serve one master.

Genesis 39

Genesis 39

Getting back to Joseph who had been sold by his own brothers to the Ishmaelites—he had been taken to Egypt and bought by Potiphar who worked for Pharaoh. God helped Joseph and put him in such a place that he became a trusted advisor in the house of Potiphar. Potiphar was no dummy and saw that Joseph was a favorite of God since everything he touched seemed to be blessed. While Joseph was in charge of his home, he also prospered.

After some time, Potiphar's wife took an interest in Joseph and she propositioned him. Joseph, being a Godly man, rejected her. Since hell hath no fury like a woman scorned, she lied about Joseph and told her husband that he tried to take advantage of her. However, God was with Joseph, and though he was sent to the king's prison, he found favor in the eyes of the warden. The warden put Joseph in charge of the other prisoners and trusted him because he also saw that the Lord was with Joseph and blessed in all he did.

Even though he was sent to prison unfairly, God still found a way to bless Joseph. Some of us are in our own type of prison, but if we look to God and trust in Him, He will find a way to bless us and keep us in peace for the duration.

GENESIS 40

Genesis 40

While Joseph was still in prison, two others joined him. The cupbearer and the baker did something to irritate the pharaoh, and he had them thrown into prison. The captain of the guard assigned them to Joseph. After some time, they each had a disturbing dream on the same night. Joseph was able to interpret their dreams with God's help.

This is how Joseph interpreted the cupbearer's dream: Within three days, he would be restored to his former position and would again put Pharaoh's cup in his hand. Joseph asked the cupbearer to put in a good word for him to the pharaoh to get him released from his undeserved imprisonment.

This is how Joseph interpreted the baker's dream: Within three days, Pharaoh would lift off his head, hang him on a tree, and the birds would eat his flesh. Yikes! There wasn't much point in asking this man to put in a good word for him with the pharaoh, and the cupbearer forgot all about him until two years later.

GENESIS 41

Genesis 41

After two years passed, Pharaoh had two dreams that no one could properly interpret. That's when the cupbearer finally remembered Joseph. So, the pharaoh sent for Joseph and asked him if he could interpret dreams. Joseph answered with an astounding "no", but told him that God would give him answers.

With God's help, Joseph interpreted Pharaoh's dreams to mean that seven years of great abundance would come to Egypt followed by seven years of famine. Joseph was given a plan by God on exactly what Egypt should do, so the pharaoh placed Joseph in charge of not only the food supply in Egypt, but also his palace. The whole land of Egypt would submit to Joseph except for the pharaoh himself, who admitted that only with respect to the throne would he be greater than Joseph. The pharaoh put all his faith in Joseph because he could see there was no one as wise and discerning as him, while Joseph put all his faith in God to guide and direct him.

Pharaoh gave Joseph his very own signet ring and dressed him in robes of fine linen. He put a gold chain around his neck and had him ride in a chariot as second-in-command. He changed his name to Zaphenath-Paneah and gave him a bride, Asenath, daughter of Potiphera, priest of On. Joseph was thirty years old when he was put into power.

During the first seven years, Joseph collected the abundant grain that was beyond measure, and he and his wife had two sons, Manasseh and Ephraim. When the seven years of famine came, the people of Egypt cried to the pharaoh, and he sent them to Joseph who was able to sell grain to them through the abundance he had stored. People also came from other countries to buy grain from Egypt because the famine was so severe all across the world. This is how Joseph's brothers came to be in Egypt.

As we will soon find out, the Lord really does work in mysterious ways, and undoubtedly, His timing is not the same as ours. Joseph had to go through many trials during his years of waiting for God's plan to happen, but he never rejected God. Joseph kept his faith, and God rewarded him, even through the difficult years, giving him small victories in the troubled times. God eventually lifted him up into a high position which would ultimately give him the ability to help the very same brothers who once hated him enough to sell him into slavery.

Ask yourself this question: If you were put in charge of the health and safety of people who once treated you horribly, what would you do? What would God want you to do? We will soon find out what Joseph does in this exact situation.

GENESIS 42

Genesis 42

During the drought, which had spread to the land of Canaan, Jacob heard there was grain in Egypt and sent ten of his sons there to purchase some; however, he kept his youngest son home. Benjamin was Jacob's son by Rachel, the love of his life, Joseph's only full-blooded brother. Jacob had lost Joseph, he'd lost Rachel, and he didn't want to chance losing their only remaining child, so he kept him home.

Jacob's sons went to the governor of the land to buy grain. They didn't recognize their brother Joseph, but he recognized them and treated them harshly, though he kept his identity secret. Joseph accused them of being spies. They denied the charges and explained who they were. They were ten of the twelve sons of one man. One son was at home with their father. The other son was no more. Joseph dealt with them harshly and would not let them leave until their youngest brother came to Egypt. Joseph put his brothers in prison.

On the third day, he showed mercy and sent them home with their grain and instructions to bring Benjamin back with them. He also required one of the brothers to remain in jail until their return. They believed they were being punished for what they had done to their little brother. Reuben lashed out at his brothers. *Didn't I tell you not to harm our brother? Now we will pay the price!* Joseph overheard Rueben's comments and turned away and cried. He knew then that Rueben had tried to help him so long ago when his other brothers sold him into slavery. He took Simeon, who was the violent one, and bound him in front of his brothers and sent him to prison to wait their return. Then he ordered his men to fill their bags with grain, provisions for their journey, and the silver the brothers used to pay for the grain. When Jacob's sons stopped for the night, they checked their packs and realized the silver was there. They panicked!

Jacob was not happy about it either. He blamed his sons for the loss of Joseph, the loss of Simeon, and he didn't want them to take Benjamin. Jacob was having his own little pity party. *Everything is against me!* Reuben offered to take full responsibility for Benjamin, even offering up his own sons as security, but Jacob wouldn't budge, at least not until they ran out of grain again.

Genesis 43

Genesis 43

When they ran out of grain, Jacob tried sending his sons back to Egypt, but Judah reminded him they were instructed not to come back without their brother Benjamin. Judah promised Jacob he would take care of Benjamin, and Jacob gave in.

Jacob sent his sons to Egypt with gifts for the leader of the land in hopes he would release Simeon and leave his other sons unharmed. He also sent double the amount of silver to pay back the amount they somehow unknowingly brought home with them the last time.

When Joseph saw Benjamin, his full brother, he planned a big dinner for them all. His brothers however, were still afraid of him. They pleaded with Joseph's steward who eased their worries and brought Simeon out to them.

At the dinner, Jacob's sons presented Joseph with gifts and bowed down to him. Joseph inquired of their father, his father. As he looked about and laid eyes on Benjamin, he became emotionally overwhelmed and had to excuse himself to cry in private. When he regained control over his emotions, he came back and they sat down to dinner. Dinner was served first to Joseph, then to his brothers, then to the Egyptians, for Hebrews and Egyptians did not dine together. The brothers were astonished to see they were sat according to their age. They also noticed Benjamin was given five times the portion of food they were given. Though they were confused, they all drank and feasted freely.

GENESIS 44

Genesis 44

When it was time for his brothers to return home, Joseph told the steward of his house to put an abundance of food in his brother's sacks and also their silver. He also told him to put his own silver cup in Benjamin's pack. Joseph was setting a trap for them, but his ultimate goal was not for harm. The next morning, Joseph's men caught up to Jacob's sons and searched their packs, accusing them of repaying good with evil. When the silver cup was found in Benjamin's pack, the brothers tore their clothes and returned to the city.

When they reached Joseph's house, they threw themselves at his mercy. Joseph claimed to know the truth by divination, which he most likely didn't practice. He wanted to keep Benjamin with him as his slave for punishment and send the others back home, but Judah stepped up and explained Jacob's emotional ties to Benjamin, especially after losing his favored son Joseph. So, Judah offered to take the place of Benjamin because he could not bear his father's broken heart.

GENESIS 45

Genesis 45

At this point, Joseph loses it. He cannot conceal his identity any longer. He sends away all his men and then reveals himself to his brothers. They were shocked. Joseph begged them not to be distressed, for he did not place any blame on his brothers. He believed it was his fate by God to end up in Egypt in order to save his family during this drought. He tells them to go get Jacob and to get their families and move them to Goshen, near to Joseph for the duration of the drought so they could survive. He and Benjamin threw their arms around each other and wept.

Pharaoh was delighted about Joseph's brothers and welcomed them with open arms promising the best of what Egypt had to offer. Joseph sent them on their way with new clothes and provisions, giving even more to Benjamin. As they were leaving he told them not to argue on the way. You know brothers. They tend to do that.

When they arrived back in Canaan, they told their father all that had happened. At first he didn't believe them, but he was soon convinced that his beloved son was really alive. His spirit revived and he made plans to go to his son.

GENESIS 46

Genesis 46

Jacob began the journey to see his beloved son. On the way, he stopped at Beersheba to offer sacrifices to the God of his father. That night, God spoke to him, telling him not to fear, that He would be with him, make him successful there, and someday bring him back home. He also assured Jacob that Joseph would be the one to close his eyes (at his death). Jacob took his entire family and all his possessions to Egypt.

Jacob sent Judah ahead to get directions to Goshen which was the land Joseph promised him, and Joseph was there to welcome his father when he arrived. Joseph threw his arms around his father and wept. He also gave his brothers instructions about what to say to Pharoah—that they were shepherds and had brought their livestock with them. This way Pharoah would allow them to live separately in Goshen, which was lush and ripe for livestock. Since the Egyptians looked down upon shepherds and didn't want to be near them, this would ensure they would be sent there.

GENESIS 47

Genesis 47

Joseph took five of his brothers to present them before the pharaoh. They did as he told them and the pharaoh not only gave them the land of Goshen to settle in, but he also put them in charge of his own livestock. Then Joseph brought in his father, and Jacob blessed the pharaoh. Upon inquiry, Jacob revealed to the pharaoh his age of 130 years, which he described as few and difficult. Joseph gave his family provisions and settled them in the land of Goshen which later became known as the district of Ramses.

The famine grew worse. The people of Egypt had used all their money to buy grain, so Joseph made a deal with them. He would accept their livestock as payment. When their livestock ran out, he accepted their land as payment. So, Joseph bought all the land in Egypt for the pharaoh and reduced the people to servitude. They would be servants on the land they sold. The only exception was to the priests because Pharaoh gave them their food and they had no need to sell their land.

Now that the people were in servitude, Joseph gave them seed to plant with the condition that they would give one-fifth of their crops to the pharaoh. The people were so desperate for food they gave up everything they owned including their freedom. This is a lesson we should learn in our own time. People are so desperate for health and safety that they seem to be willing to give up everything. Once the deal is made, there is no going back, as the people in Egypt soon found out.

As for Jacob and his family, they were firmly established in Egypt, in the land of Goshen, and they were fruitful and multiplied greatly. Jacob lived in Egypt for seventeen years. When the time of his death grew near, he made Joseph swear to bury him with his fathers, not in Egypt.

GENESIS 48

Genesis 48

When Jacob fell ill, Joseph took his sons, Manasseh and Ephraim, to see his father. Jacob gathered his strength to sit up in bed to see his beloved son and to tell him the story about when God spoke to him in Canaan and blessed him and promised him that his descendants would be fruitful and multiply and become their own community which would have that land as their everlasting possession.

Jacob blessed Joseph's two sons as if they were his own. However, Jacob insisted on giving the greater blessing to Ephraim who was not the firstborn. Joseph questioned him about it, but Jacob knew what he was doing. The blessing he bestowed on Ephraim: his descendants would greatly multiply. Manasseh would receive a smaller blessing in that he would also be great, but Ephraim's descendants would be greater in numbers and would become a group of nations. Just like Jacob, the second-born, received the birthright, he was now giving Joseph's second son the greater blessing.

In Jacob's blessing, he gave the God of his fathers, the *Angel who had delivered him from harm, the glory for guiding him throughout his life. Jacob assured Joseph that God would be with him and lead him back to the land of his fathers. Then he gave Joseph, the one who was over his brothers, the ridge of land which he (Jacob) had taken from the Amorites with sword and bow.

*The Angel of the Lord is often believed to be Jesus.

GENESIS 49

Genesis 49

Jacob called all of his sons to him and gave this prophecy over them and their descendants:

1. Reuben, his first born, excelling in honor and power, would no longer excel due to the sin of sleeping with Jacob's concubine Bilhah.

2. & 3. Simeon and Levi, due to their level of violence and cruelty, would be scattered in Israel.

4. Judah would be praised by his brothers, and their sons would bow down to him. The obedience of the nations would be his. (Jesus is a descendant of Judah).

5. Zebulun would live by the sea and become a haven for ships.

6. Issachar would end up submitting to forced labor.

7. Dan would provide justice for his people as a viper that bites at horses' heels.

8. Gad would be attacked and he would retaliate.

9. Asher's food would be rich and provide delicacies fit for the king.

10. Naphtali would be a doe set free who would have beautiful fawns.

11. Joseph, a fruitful vine, would be attacked by bitter archers but would remain steady because of help from the Lord.

12. Benjamin would be a ravenous wolf, devouring his prey and dividing the plunder.

These would be the tribes of Israel.

Before Jacob died, he instructed his sons to bury him with his fathers in the cave where Abraham and Sarah were buried, where Isaac and Rebekah were buried, and where his wife Leah was buried. Remember that Rachel had died before reaching their destination and had to be buried elsewhere.

GENESIS 50

Genesis 50

Joseph wept over his father's death then had the physicians embalm him. This was something the Egyptians did. After all the days of mourning, Joseph received permission from the pharaoh to go bury his father in Canaan. Joseph, his brothers, and Pharaoh's officials and dignitaries accompanied him on the journey. When they approached the Jordan, they observed a seventy day period of mourning. The Canaanites thought they were all Egyptians. After burying his father, they returned to Egypt.

At this point, Joseph's brothers are now afraid of retaliation against them for selling their brother into slavery so long ago. They have no faith that their brother forgave them, so once again Joseph had to reassure them that all was well. It seems they worried for nothing, like we often do.

Joseph stayed in Egypt until he died at the age of 110. Before he died he made his brothers promise that when the Lord brought them out of Egypt into their own land, they would take his body with them and bury him in the land promised to Abraham, Isaac, and Jacob. When he died, he was embalmed and placed in a coffin in Egypt to await his final burying place.

This is the end of Genesis, which is only the beginning.

About the Author

Walker Lane graduated from Sam Houston State University with a Bachelor's Degree in English, minoring in History. After teaching for fifteen years, she decided to pursue her love of writing which stemmed from a childhood full of daydreams. As a teacher, she learned to organize those daydreams into stories.

Her writing career began as a small child with her first poem titled "A Friend" (written on a "Hello Kitty" notepad), and continued on through high school writing articles and poems for the school newspaper, and on through the debut of her first novel *Remember Me*.

Today she continues writing a Christian Blog and is currently working on her next novel. She is a devoted wife, mother, and Christian residing in Texas. Visit her website at Walker-Lane.com, on Facebook at facebook.com/walker.lane.73, or https://www.facebook.com/Walkerswritings, on Twitter at Walker Lane @WalkerLane1.

ALSO BY WALKER LANE:

Remember Me

Walker Lane's Book of Easy-Peasy Recipes

https://walker-lane.com

Made in the USA
Columbia, SC
24 August 2023